GW00419276

Contents

Please log our songs on your CWCL or CCL copy report

1

At 'Out of the Ark' it has always been our conviction that songs have a remarkable and invaluable capacity both to harness children's interest and enthusiasm, and to facilitate learning way beyond the remit of the music curriculum. We believe this to be supremely true in the learning of languages.

Chantons! Tous Les Jours was born out of a response to the government strategy which set out to make language learning an entitlement for every child at KS2 by the year 2010. In a climate of already over-stretched teachers, with few language specialists, we decided to publish a simple but dynamic, interactive resource, which would appeal to both teachers, non-specialists and children alike – and that would also offer something more than other similar publications.

We have written 12 simple but catchy songs, specifically intended to introduce key vocabulary and core topic areas, with a good dose of fun! Each of these is accompanied by lively interactive whiteboard activities, which introduce the key ideas and vocabulary used in each song. Our Teacher's Book includes everything you could need (without ANY prior knowledge of the language!) with photocopiable worksheets, planned extension activities and vocabulary listings – and to enhance the singing and learning experience, we have incorporated our Words on Screen™ lyric projection system. We are confident and proud to present a resource that will make language learning both accessible and enjoyable for everyone.

Chantons! Tous Les Jours – **the innovative, fail-safe and fun method of introducing children to the French language.**

For each song in this *Chantons! Tous Les Jours* collection, you have the following resources:

Song information – this gives some basic facts about the song, along with hints and tips for teaching it.

Audio track – this is recorded as a vocal performance (using native French voices) and also as a backing track. We would suggest playing the vocal track to the children a few times before you begin teaching the song. This way, they will pick up the melody and rhythm naturally and be halfway there to singing it!

An interactive lesson – this is a really fun and exciting way for the children to learn some essential vocabulary used in the song. They are able to hear words and phrases, spoken in native French accents, whilst also constructing sentences and revising words they've learnt already. To use, just select the song you are working on from the CD ROM, and the rest should be easy to follow using the instructions given on the lesson page. The lesson pages lead straight into the Words on Screen™ program.

Words on Screen™ – the lyrics for the song are displayed on your screen or interactive whiteboard, and each line is highlighted as it is sung. You can choose to play the track with or without the vocals, pause it, or skip back and forth between verses, so this is an ideal tool to use both for rehearsal and performance.

Key and further vocabulary – we've listed all the key words and phrases that will be learnt through the song on the Song Information page.

Other activities – every song has some simple extra activities given as suggestions to help embed the necessary vocabulary. These can be found on the Song Information page.

A lyric sheet – this can be photocopied, or printed from the pdf given on the CD ROM.

A photocopiable activity sheet – designed to reinforce the vocabulary taught for the song. Ideal for a quiet ten minutes' lesson-time, or to be used for homework. (These are also given as PDFs on the CD ROM – for you to print as necessary.)

Sheet music – for those of you that love to play as you teach, we have supplied the melody line along with chords and lyrics. Great if you want to practise the song using piano or guitar.

Un, deux, trois
One, two, three

About the song

This is a fairly simple song that's great for learning to count in French. You'll hear that the rhythm changes in verse two, so the words fall on different beats. It may take a while to get it, but work at it and it will really help embed the numbers in your brain!

Also, watch out as the track picks up pace, getting faster the second time through.

Key vocabulary

un············one
deux···········two
trois············three
quatre·········four
cinq············five
six·············six
sept············seven
huit············eight
neuf············nine
dix·············ten

Je sais compter·······I know how to count
Comme ça!···········like that!

Further vocabulary

onze···············eleven
douze·············twelve
treize·············thirteen

J'ai neuf/dix/onze ans·······I am 9/10/11 years old

1 2 3 4 5 6
7 8 9 10

Other activities

When the children are familiar with counting confidently from one to ten, experiment with their understanding. For example:

• When the teacher, or a child, calls out a number in French, that number of children stand up. (Put children into groups of ten or more before you begin. Each group can do the activity at the same time.)

• Try learning to say the numbers in descending order from 10 down to 1. With 10 children sitting roughly in a row, assign them a French number each, from 1-10. Have them stand up (and then sit down again) as they say their number. Get them used to doing this in ascending order first, and then with greater speed. Once they've mastered this, start at the other end of the line, with 10 going down to 1. Once the class has heard the pattern a few times, they will be able to join in: 'dix, neuf, huit, sept, six …'.

Un, deux, trois

1 Un, deux, trois,
   Quatre, cinq, six,
   Sept, huit, neuf et dix.
   Un, deux, trois,
   Quatre, cinq, six,
   Sept, huit, neuf et dix.

One, two, three,
Four, five, six,
Seven, eight, nine and ten.
One, two, three,
Four, five, six,
Seven, eight, nine and ten.

CHORUS

Je sais compter, je sais compter,
Je sais compter, un, deux, trois.
Je sais compter, je sais compter,
Je sais compter, comme ça!

I know how to count, I know how to count,
I know how to count, one, two, three.
I know how to count, I know how to count,
I know how to count, like that!

2 Un, deux, trois, quatre, cinq,
   Six, sept, huit, neuf, dix.
   Un, deux, trois, quatre, cinq,
   Six, sept, huit, neuf, dix.

One, two, three, four, five,
Six, seven, eight, nine, ten.
One, two, three, four, five,
Six, seven, eight, nine, ten.

CHORUS

Repeat whole song, getting gradually faster, with double chorus to finish.

Words and Music by Mark and Helen Johnson
© 2010 Out of the Ark Ltd, Middlesex TW12 2HD
CCLI Song No. 5703452

Lundi, mardi, mercredi
Monday, Tuesday, Wednesday

About the song

This song has three main sections: the first simply teaches the days of the week; the second covers the weekend, and includes a possible harmony; the third ('What day is it today?') also gives scope for vocal harmony should you wish to include it. You can make this as simple or as complicated as you like!

Key vocabulary

lundi ·············· *Monday*

mardi ·············· *Tuesday*

mercredi ·········· *Wednesday*

jeudi ·············· *Thursday*

vendredi ·········· *Friday*

samedi ············ *Saturday*

dimanche ········· *Sunday*

NB – days of the week in French don't use capital letters.

le weekend ·································· *the weekend*

J'aime beaucoup le weekend ········ *I really like the weekend*

C'est quel jour aujourd'hui? ········· *What day is it today?*

Aujourd'hui c'est ····················· *Today it's*

Other activities

Work in pairs using the information from the children's activity calendars (see activity sheet on page 29). One child describes in English what happens to them on a particular day, for example, 'Today I go swimming', then asks 'C'est quel jour aujourd'hui?' Their partner then uses the first child's calendar to look and answer, 'Aujourd'hui c'est ...'.

Lundi, mardi, mercredi

1   Lundi, mardi, mercredi,
    Jeudi, vendredi.
    Lundi, mardi, mercredi,
    Jeudi, vendredi.
    (Répétez)

    Monday, Tuesday, Wednesday,
    Thursday, Friday.
    Monday, Tuesday, Wednesday,
    Thursday, Friday.

2   J'aime beaucoup le weekend,
    Samedi et dimanche.
    J'aime beaucoup le weekend,
    Samedi et dimanche.
    (Répétez)

    I really like the weekend,
    Saturday and Sunday.
    I really like the weekend,
    Saturday and Sunday.

3   C'est quel jour aujourd'hui?
    Aujourd'hui c'est mercredi/lundi*.
    C'est quel jour aujourd'hui?
    Aujourd'hui c'est mercredi/lundi.
    (Répétez)

    What day is it today?
    Today it's Wednesday/Monday.*
    What day is it today?
    Today it's Wednesday/Monday.

Repeat whole song through once more.

* Insert whichever day of the week it is today.

Words and Music by Mark and Helen Johnson
© 2010 Out of the Ark Ltd, Middlesex TW12 2HD
CCLI Song No. 5703469

Comment t'appelles-tu?

What's your name?

About the song

The number of syllables in a child's name will affect the rhythm of how they finish the sentence 'Je m'appelle ...' Listen to the song first with the children to see how the examples we have included are sung. Then discuss the different names in the class and try slotting them into the song. Once the children are confident, you can pick a few of them to sing the reply to the question, 'Comment t'appelles-tu?' throughout the song.

Key vocabulary

Comment t'appelles-tu?··············*What's your name?*
Je m'appelle······································*My name is*
Ça va?···*How are you?*
Ça va bien, merci···························*I'm very well, thank you*

Other activities

- Get the children to draw a detailed picture of themselves on the activity sheet supplied. Before they label it with their own name, share the pictures for the whole class to see. Can they recognise who they are? Let the class guess. The child whose picture it is owns it by saying 'Je m'appelle ...'.

- Write each of the children's names on pieces of card/paper. Put them into groups of 1/2/3/4 syllable names and practise saying and listening to 'Je m'appelle ...'.

- In pairs, practise the questions in the key vocabulary list. Then swap over.

Comment t'appelles-tu?

CHORUS

Comment t'appelles-tu?	*What's your name?*
Comment t'appelles-tu?	*What's your name?*
Comment t'appelles-tu?	*What's your name?*
Dis-moi!	*Tell me!*
(Répétez)	

1
Je m'appelle Hélène,	*My name is Helen,*
Je m'appelle Hélène,	*My name is Helen,*
Je m'appelle Hélène,	*My name is Helen,*
Et toi?	*And you?*

2
Je m'appelle Jacques,	*My name is Jack,*
Je m'appelle Jacques,	*My name is Jack,*
Je m'appelle Jacques,	*My name is Jack,*
Comment ça va?	*How are you?*

Ça va très bien, merci, merci,	*I'm very well, thank you, thank you,*
Ça va très bien, ça va très bien!	*I'm very well, I'm very well!*
(Répétez)	

CHORUS

3
Je m'appelle Isabelle,	*My name is Isabelle,*
Je m'appelle Isabelle,	*My name is Isabelle,*
Je m'appelle Isabelle,	*My name is Isabelle,*
Et toi?	*And you?*

4
Je m'appelle Emmanuel,	*My name is Emmanuel,*
Je m'appelle Emmanuel,	*My name is Emmanuel,*
Je m'appelle Emmanuel,	*My name is Emmanuel,*
Comment ça va?	*How are you?*

Ça va très bien, merci, merci,	*I'm very well, thank you, thank you,*
Ça va très bien, ça va très bien!	*I'm very well, I'm very well!*
(Répétez)	

Words and Music by Mark and Helen Johnson
© 2010 Out of the Ark Ltd, Middlesex TW12 2HD
CCLI Song No. 5703476

Dans ma famille

In my family

About the song

This very simple song uses core vocabulary about the family, with lots of helpful repetition. Once you have mastered the basic melody with understanding of the text, you can try adding a simple harmony.

Key vocabulary

ma mère* ·················· *my mother*
mon père ·················· *my father*
ma sœur ·················· *my sister*
mon frère ·················· *my brother*
et moi ·················· *and me*

dans ma famille ·················· *in my family*
nous sommes cinq ···· *there are five of us*
voilà ·················· *there you are*

Further vocabulary

ma grand-mère ·················· *my grandma*
mon grand-père ·················· *my grandad*
ma tante ·················· *my aunt*
mon oncle ·················· *my uncle*

ma famille

Other activities

Help the children to say some simple sentences about their family, including how many brothers/sisters they have, for example:

J'ai un(e)/deux/trois/quatre sœur(s)/frère(s) ··*I have 1/2/3/4 sister(s)/brother(s)***
Dans ma famille nous sommes ·················· *In my family there are*
deux/trois/quatre/cinq/six/sept, etc. ·················· *2/3/4/5/6/7, etc.*

* Many children will use the more informal terms of 'maman' (mum) and 'papa' (dad).

** When using un(e), remember to select the correct gender for sister (une) or brother (un).

Dans ma famille

1   Dans ma famille, dans ma famille,   *In my family, in my family,*
     Dans ma famille nous sommes cinq.   *In my family there are five of us.*
     Dans ma famille, dans ma famille,   *In my family, in my family,*
     Dans ma famille nous sommes cinq.   *In my family there are five of us.*

CHORUS
     Ma mère, mon père,   *My mother, my father,*
     Ma soeur, mon frère et moi.   *My sister, my brother and me.*
     Ma mère, mon père,   *My mother, my father,*
     Ma soeur, mon frère et moi,   *My sister, my brother and me,*
     Voilà!   *There you are!*

2   Dans ma famille, dans ma famille,   *In my family, in my family,*
     Dans ma famille nous sommes cinq.   *In my family there are five of us.*
     Dans ma famille, dans ma famille,   *In my family, in my family,*
     Dans ma famille nous sommes cinq.   *In my family there are five of us.*

CHORUS
     Ma mère, mon père,   *My mother, my father,*
     Ma soeur, mon frère et moi.   *My sister, my brother and me.*
     Ma mère, mon père,   *My mother, my father,*
     Ma soeur, mon frère et moi.   *My sister, my brother and me.*

     Ma mère, mon père,   *My mother, my father,*
     Ma soeur, mon frère et moi.   *My sister, my brother and me.*
     Ma mère, mon père,   *My mother, my father,*
     Ma soeur, mon frère et moi,   *My sister, my brother and me,*
     Voilà!   *There you are!*

Words and Music by Mark and Helen Johnson
© 2010 Out of the Ark Ltd, Middlesex TW12 2HD
CCLI Song No. 5703490

Qu'est-ce que c'est?

What's that?

About the song

We've used this song to highlight lots of the objects found in and around the classroom, but you can re-use it to help with other nouns you might be learning.

Try splitting the class into two groups, one singing the chorus, asking, 'Qu'est-ce que c'est?' and the other group replying with the verses.

Key vocabulary

Qu'est-ce que c'est?	*what is it?*
Dis-le moi	*Tell me*
S'il te plaît*	*please*
C'est un(e)	*it's a*
Une trousse	*a pencil-case*
Un stylo	*a pen*
Une gomme	*a rubber*
Un livre	*a book*

Further vocabulary

Un crayon	*a pencil*
Une règle	*a ruler*
Une table	*a table*
Une chaise	*a chair*
Une porte	*a door*

* When talking to an adult, 'S'il vous plaît' should be used.'

Other activities

• Practise the key vocabulary questions in pairs. Then swap over.

• Use a simple French dictionary to find out the French words for key things around the classroom. Make labels and attach them around the room, or create a simple classroom picture dictionary.

Qu'est-ce que c'est?

CHORUS

Qu'est-ce que c'est?	*What is it?*
Qu'est-ce que c'est?	*What is it?*
Dis-le moi	*Tell me*
S'il te plaît!	*Please!*
(Répétez)	

1   C'est une trousse, c'est une trousse,   *It's a pencil case, it's a pencil case,*
C'est une trousse, je dirais!   *It's a pencil case, I would say!*
(Répétez)

CHORUS

2   C'est un stylo, c'est un stylo,   *It's a pen, it's a pen,*
C'est un stylo, je dirais!   *It's a pen, I would say!*
(Répétez)

CHORUS

3   C'est une gomme, c'est une gomme,   *It's a rubber, it's a rubber,*
C'est une gomme, je dirais!   *It's a rubber, I would say!*
(Répétez)

CHORUS

4   C'est un crayon, c'est un crayon,   *It's a pencil, it's a pencil,*
C'est un crayon, je dirais!   *It's a pencil, I would say!*
(Répétez)

CHORUS

Words and Music by Mark and Helen Johnson
© 2010 Out of the Ark Ltd, Middlesex TW12 2HD
CCLI Song No. 5703517

De quelle couleur?
What colour?

About the song

This Caribbean-style song is a good fun introduction to basic colours as well as some fruits and vegetables – learning with a bit of a lilt! There's plenty of scope to extend the experience by introducing a broader vocabulary.

Key vocabulary

de quelle couleur?·····*what colour?*
les bananes·············*the bananas*
les tomates············*the tomatoes*
les oignons············*the onions*
les légumes···········*the vegetables*

jaune··········*yellow*
rouge··········*red*
vert(e)··········*green*

Further vocabulary

blanc(he)*····*white*
noir(e)·········*black*
bleu············*blue*
orange·······*orange*
marron·······*brown*
rose············*pink*

de quelle couleur sont les bananes?···*what colour are the bananas?*
la couleur des bananes est jaune········*the colour of the bananas is yellow*

* Bracketed version equals feminine form.

Other activities

- Use a simple French dictionary to look up some other foods that can be linked with the further vocabulary colours. Compile a list with each one:
    La couleur des citrons est jaune
    La couleur des framboises est rose, etc.

- Make a chart showing each of the different colours, labelled in French. By each colour list all the food that fits that colour category – also in French.

De quelle couleur?

1   De quelle couleur, de quelle couleur,   *What colour, what colour,*
    De quelle couleur sont les bananes?   *What colour are bananas?*
    De quelle couleur, de quelle couleur,   *What colour, what colour,*
    De quelle couleur sont les bananes?   *What colour are bananas?*

    La couleur des bananes est jaune,   *The colour of bananas is yellow,*
    La couleur des bananes est jaune.   *The colour of bananas is yellow,*
    De quelle couleur, de quelle couleur?   *What colour, what colour?*
    La couleur des bananes est jaune.   *The colour of bananas is yellow.*

2   De quelle couleur, de quelle couleur,   *What colour, what colour,*
    De quelle couleur sont les tomates?   *What colour are tomatoes?*
    De quelle couleur, de quelle couleur,   *What colour, what colour,*
    De quelle couleur sont les tomates?   *What colour are tomatoes?*

    La couleur des tomates est rouge   *The colour of tomatoes is red,*
    La couleur des tomates est rouge.   *The colour of tomatoes is red,*
    De quelle couleur, de quelle couleur?   *What colour, what colour?*
    La couleur des tomates est rouge.   *The colour of tomatoes is red.*

3   De quelle couleur, de quelle couleur,   *What colour, what colour,*
    De quelle couleur sont les oignons? Etc. *What colour are onions? Etc.*

    La couleur des oignons est blanche, etc. *The colour of onions is white, etc.*

4   De quelle couleur, de quelle couleur,   *What colour, what colour,*
    De quelle couleur sont les légumes? Etc. *What colour are vegetables? Etc.*

    La couleur des légumes est verte,* etc.   *The colour of vegetables is green, etc.*

Words and Music by Mark and Helen Johnson
© 2010 Out of the Ark Ltd, Middlesex TW12 2HD
CCLI Song No. 5703524

Mon petit ami bizarre
My funny little friend

About the song

This fun song includes a good deal of vocabulary. As it features numbers as well as body parts, we suggest that you teach 'Un, deux, trois' before you try tackling this one, to help establish the numbers first.

Key vocabulary

mon ami	*my friend*
mon petit ami	*my little friend*
mon petit ami bizarre	*my funny/strange little friend*
Avez-vous rencontré mon petit ami bizarre?	*Have you met my funny little friend?*

deux	*two*	**les têtes (f)**	*heads*
trois	*three*	**les jambes (f)**	*legs*
quatre	*four*	**les bras (m)**	*arms*
cinq	*five*	**beaucoup de bras**	*lots of arms*
six	*six*	**les yeux (m)**	*eyes*
sept	*seven*	**l'oeil (m)**	*the eye*
huit	*eight*	**les oreilles (f)**	*ears*
neuf	*nine*	**les bouches (f)**	*mouths*
		les dents (f)	*teeth*
		les mains (f)	*hands*
		les pieds (m)	*feet*
		grand	*big*

Mon petit ami bizarre

CHORUS

Avez-vous rencontré	*Have you met*
Mon petit ami bizarre?*	*My funny little friend?*
Avez-vous rencontré	*Have you met*
Mon petit ami bizarre?	*My funny little friend?*

1
Il a deux têtes et trois jambes,	*He has two heads and three legs,*
Il a beaucoup de bras.	*He has lots of arms.*
Il a quatre bouches et cinq oreilles,	*He has four mouths and five ears,*
Mon petit ami bizarre!	*My funny little friend!*

CHORUS

2
Il a six yeux et sept dents,	*He has six eyes and seven teeth,*
Il a beaucoup de bras.	*He has lots of arms.*
Il a huit mains et neuf grands pieds,	*He has eight hands and nine big feet,*
Mon petit ami bizarre!	*My funny little friend!*

CHORUS

3
Il a deux têtes et trois jambes,	*He has two heads and three legs,*
Il a beaucoup de bras.	*He has lots of arms.*
Il a quatre bouches et cinq oreilles,	*He has four mouths and five ears,*
Mon petit ami bizarre!	*My funny little friend!*

4
Il a six yeux et sept dents,	*He has six eyes and seven teeth,*
Il a beaucoup de bras.	*He has lots of arms.*
Il a huit mains et neuf grands pieds,	*He has eight hands and nine big feet,*
Mon petit ami bizarre!	*My funny little friend!*
Mon petit ami bizarre!	*My funny little friend!*

* Or 'mon petit copain bizarre' *(funny little friend)*

Words and Music by Mark and Helen Johnson
© 2010 Out of the Ark Ltd, Middlesex TW12 2HD
CCLI Song No. 5703531

Les animaux
The animals

About the song

This song really isn't difficult, but it features quite a lot of vocabulary. It's well worth putting in a bit of time learning the key words/expressions before you tackle the melody. The interactive lessons on the CD ROM should help with this.

Key vocabulary

les animaux	*the animals*
une souris	*a mouse*
un lapin	*a rabbit*
un chat	*a cat*
blanc(he) et noir(e)	*white and black*
un chien	*a dog*
un cheval	*a horse*
un dauphin	*a dolphin*
Je voudrais avoir	*I would like to have*
Je voudrais surtout	*I would especially like*
De tous les animaux dans le monde	*Of all the animals in the world*

Other activities

Use a simple French dictionary to look up the words for other animals not included in the song (e.g. farm animals, zoo animals, personal favourites). Make a collage of animal pictures with the English and French words underneath each animal.

18

Les animaux

1   Je voudrais avoir une souris,   *I would like to have a mouse,*
    Je voudrais avoir un lapin.   *I would like to have a rabbit.*
    Je voudrais avoir un chat blanc et noir,   *I would like to have a white and black cat,*
    Je voudrais surtout un chien!   *I would especially like a dog!*

CHORUS
    De tous les animaux dans le monde   *Of all the animals in the world*
    Je voudrais surtout un chien.   *I would especially like a dog!*
    (Répétez)

2   Je voudrais avoir un cheval,   *I would like to have a horse,*
    Je voudrais avoir un dauphin.   *I would like to have a dolphin.*
    Je voudrais avoir un chat blanc et noir,   *I would like to have a white and black cat,*
    Je voudrais surtout un chien!   *I would especially like a dog!*

CHORUS

3   Je voudrais avoir une souris,   *I would like to have a mouse,*
    Je voudrais avoir un lapin.   *I would like to have a rabbit.*
    Je voudrais avoir un chat blanc et noir,   *I would like to have a white and black cat,*
    Je voudrais surtout un chien!   *I would especially like a dog!*
    Je voudrais avoir un chat blanc et noir,   *I would like to have a white and black cat,*
    Je voudrais surtout un chien!   *I would especially like a dog!*

Words and Music by Mark and Helen Johnson
© 2010 Out of the Ark Ltd, Middlesex TW12 2HD
CCLI Song No. 5703548

Tous les jours
Every day

About the song

This song features the days of the week and introduces simple reflexive verbs.
We recommend you learn the song 'Lundi, mardi, mercredi' before you try this one.

Key vocabulary

tous les jours ······ *every day*
Je me lève ·········· *I get up*
Je me lave ·········· *I get washed*
Je me coiffe ········ *I do my hair*
Je me couche ····· *I go to bed*

lundi ·············· *Monday*
mardi ············· *Tuesday*
mercredi ········· *Wednesday*
jeudi ·············· *Thursday*
vendredi ········· *Friday*
samedi ············ *Saturday*
dimanche ········· *Sunday*

Further vocabulary

Je me douche ················· *I have a shower*
Je me repose ················· *I rest*
Je me réveille ················ *I wake up*
Je me brosse les dents ····· *I brush my teeth*
Je me mouche ················· *I blow my nose*
Je m'habille ···················· *I get dressed*

Other activities

• Having learnt the song thoroughly, assign different days of the week to various children. Have them stand up swiftly (and sit down just as fast) when their day is sung in the chorus.

• Choose 7 children to stand in a line. Give them each a card with a day of the week on (in English) to hold up in front of them. Ask them to sort themselves out into the right order. Have the rest of the class call out the days of the week, in French, as each of them holds up their card in turn. Having mastered that, ask the children to re-arrange themselves into a completely different order. See if the class can remember the French words now!

• Learn the difference between the following: je me couche (I go to bed); je me douche (I have a shower); je me mouche (I blow my nose)!

Tous les jours

1   Tous les jours je me lève,
    Je me lève tous les jours.
    (Répétez)

         Every day I get up,
         I get up every day.

CHORUS
Lundi, mardi, mercredi,
Jeudi, vendredi,
Samedi, dimanche,
Tous les jours.
(Répétez)

         Monday, Tuesday, Wednesday,
         Thursday, Friday,
         Saturday, Sunday,
         Every day.

2   Tous les jours je me lave,
    Je me lave tous les jours.
    (Répétez)

         Every day I get washed,
         I get washed every day.

CHORUS

3   Tous les jours je me coiffe,
    Je me coiffe tous les jours.
    (Répétez)

         Every day I do my hair,
         I do my hair every day.

CHORUS

4   Tous les jours je me couche,
    Je me couche tous les jours.
    (Répétez)

         Every day I go to bed,
         I go to bed every day.

CHORUS

Words and Music by Mark and Helen Johnson
© 2010 Out of the Ark Ltd, Middlesex TW12 2HD
CCLI Song No. 5703555

Dans ma poche
In my pocket

About the song

This song has been written using fun rhyming vocabulary, rather than any essential first words the children may learn. It would be good to learn the song 'Un, deux, trois' before you try this one.

After you have learnt the song and sung it through with the 4 straight verses, have some fun singing it as a 3-part round. Either use the first 3 verses, or choose some of the words from the further vocabulary list to make up your own.

Key vocabulary

ma poche	*my pocket*
dans ma poche	*in my pocket*
un	*one*
deux	*two*
trois	*three*
quatre	*four*
J'ai un poisson	*I have a fish*
J'ai deux chiffons	*I have two dusters*
J'ai trois boutons	*I have three buttons*
J'ai quatre bonbons	*I have four sweets*
Quel grand poisson!	*What a big fish!*
Dans ma poche j'ai	*In my pocket I have*
C'est amusant!	*That's funny!*

Further vocabulary

cinq	*five*
six	*six*
sept	*seven*
huit	*eight*
les crayons	*pencils*
les oignons	*onions*
les ballons	*balls*

Dans ma poche

(This song also works as a round, using the first 3 verses only.)

1 Dans ma poche j'ai un poisson,
   Dans ma poche j'ai un poisson.
   Un poisson, c'est amusant!
   Oh-la-la! Quel grand poisson!

In my pocket, I have one fish,
In my pocket, I have one fish.
One fish, that's funny!
Oh-la-la! What a big fish!

2 Dans ma poche j'ai deux chiffons,
   Dans ma poche j'ai deux chiffons.
   Deux chiffons, c'est amusant!
   Oh-la-la! Quels grands chiffons!

In my pocket I have two dusters,
In my pocket I have two dusters.
Two dusters, that's funny!
Oh-la-la! What big dusters!

3 Dans ma poche j'ai trois boutons,
   Dans ma poche j'ai trois boutons.
   Trois boutons, c'est amusant!
   Oh-la-la! Quels grands boutons!

In my pocket I have three buttons,
In my pocket I have three buttons.
Three buttons, that's funny!
Oh-la-la! What big buttons!

4 Dans ma poche j'ai quatre bonbons,
   Dans ma poche j'ai quatre bonbons.
   Quatre bonbons, c'est amusant!
   Oh-la-la! Quels grands bonbons!

In my pocket I have four sweets,
In my pocket I have four sweets.
Four sweets, that's funny!
Oh-la-la! What big sweets!

Aussi....

5 cinq crayons   *five pencils*
6 six oignons   *six onions*
7 sept ballons   *seven balls*

Words and Music by Mark and Helen Johnson
© 2010 Out of the Ark Ltd, Middlesex TW12 2HD
CCLI Song No. 5703562

J'ai perdu mon chapeau!

I have lost my hat!

About the song

This is a really fun song that uses words and phrases that may be unfamiliar, but are the key to its enjoyment. Have a play around with the lyrics to create various combinations of nonsense.

Key vocabulary

mon chapeau	*my hat*
mon gâteau	*my cake*
mon bateau	*my boat*
J'ai perdu mon	*I have lost my*
J'ai lavé mon	*I have washed my*
J'ai mangé mon	*I have eaten my*
C'est vrai!	*it's true!*
C'est faux!	*it's false!*
Ce que vous dites, c'est vrai.	*What you are saying is true.*
Ce que vous dites, c'est faux.	*What you are saying is false.*
Dites qu'en pensez-vous?	*Say, what do you think?*

Other activities

- Practise using the phrases *'C'est vrai!/C'est faux!'* In pairs, one child makes up a sentence about themselves (in English). The partner has to guess whether or not they are telling the truth, and answer in French, either *'C'est vrai!'* or *'C'est faux!'*

- Make up believable and ridiculous sentences using key verbs from this song with other vocabulary you have learnt, such as classroom objects – see 'Qu'est-ce que c'est?' For example:

    J'ai mangé mon stylo.
    J'ai lavé mon livre.

J'ai perdu mon chapeau!

1   J'ai perdu mon chapeau,   *I have lost my hat,*
    J'ai lavé mon bateau,   *I have washed my boat,*
    J'ai mangé mon gâteau,   *I have eaten my cake,*
    Dites qu'en pensez-vous?   *Say, what do you think?*
    (Répétez)

CHORUS

    C'est vrai! C'est vrai!   *It's true! It's true!*
    Ce que vous dites, c'est vrai, c'est vrai!   *What you are saying is true!*
    (Répétez)

2   J'ai lavé mon gâteau,   *I have washed my cake,*
    J'ai lavé mon gâteau,   *I have washed my cake,*
    J'ai lavé mon gâteau,   *I have washed my cake,*
    Dites qu'en pensez-vous?   *Say, what do you think?*
    (Répétez)

CHORUS

    C'est faux! C'est faux!   *It's false! It's false!*
    Ce que vous dites, c'est faux, c'est faux!   *What you are saying is false!*
    (Répétez)

3   J'ai mangé mon chapeau,   *I have eaten my hat,*
    J'ai mangé mon chapeau,   *I have eaten my hat,*
    J'ai mangé mon chapeau,   *I have eaten my hat,*
    Dites qu'en pensez-vous?   *Say, what do you think?*
    (Répétez)

CHORUS

4   J'ai perdu mon bateau,   *I have lost my boat,*
    J'ai perdu mon bateau,   *I have lost my boat,*
    J'ai perdu mon bateau,   *I have lost my boat,*
    Dites qu'en pensez-vous?   *Say, what do you think?*
    (Répétez)

Words and Music by Mark and Helen Johnson
© 2010 Out of the Ark Ltd, Middlesex TW12 2HD
CCLI Song No. 5703579

Où se trouve mon parapluie?
Where's my umbrella?

About the song

This simple song introduces basic weather vocabulary as well as the core expressions connected with I like/I don't like/I really like. It features repeated rain, so take a look at the interactive lesson on the CD ROM and have some fun finding the umbrella!

Key vocabulary

il fait froid··*it's cold*
il fait chaud······································*it's hot*
aujourd'hui·······································*today*
le temps···*the weather*
le temps d'ici···································*the weather here*
J'aime···*I like*
J'aime beaucoup·······················*I really like*
Je n'aime pas·································*I don't like*
il pleut··*it's raining*
quand il pleut································*when it rains*
quelqu'un dit·································*someone says*
mon parapluie·······························*my umbrella*
Où se trouve mon parapluie?·····*Where's my umbrella?*

Further vocabulary

Quel temps fait-il (aujourd'hui)?···········
················*What's the weather like (today)?*
il fait beau··············*it's nice*
il fait mauvais·········*it's bad*
il fait très chaud·····*it's very hot*
il fait du vent··········*it's windy*
il neige····················*it's snowing*

Other Activities

- Using the vocabulary above, make some picture weather cards to illustrate each of the main weather types. Write a separate French label for each picture (e.g. il pleut). Get the children to match the pictures/words.

- Use the weather illustrations above to talk about the weather each day:

  'Quel temps fait-il aujourd'hui?'
  'Aujourd'hui, il fait froid.'

- Make a weather calendar. Display the days of the week (in French), and let the children put up the appropriate weather 'card' each day they come to school.

Où se trouve mon parapluie?

1   Il fait froid aujourd'hui,
    Je n'aime pas le temps d'ici!
    Quand il pleut, quelqu'un dit,
    'Où se trouve mon parapluie?!'

2   Il fait chaud aujourd'hui,
    J'aime beaucoup le temps d'ici!
    Quand il pleut, quelqu'un dit,
    'Où se trouve mon parapluie?'

3   Il fait froid aujourd'hui,
    Je n'aime pas le temps d'ici!
    Quand il pleut, quelqu'un dit,
    'Où se trouve mon parapluie?!'

4   Il fait chaud aujourd'hui,
    J'aime beaucoup le temps d'ici!
    Quand il pleut, quelqu'un dit,
    'Où se trouve mon parapluie?'
    'Où se trouve mon parapluie?'

It's cold today,
I don't like the weather here!
When it rains, someone says,
'Where's my umbrella?'

It's hot today,
I really like the weather here!
When it rains, someone says,
'Where's my umbrella?'

It's cold today,
I don't like the weather here!
When it rains, someone says,
'Where's my umbrella?'

It's hot today,
I really like the weather here!
When it rains, someone says,
'Where's my umbrella?'
'Where's my umbrella?'

Words and Music by Mark and Helen Johnson
© 2010 Out of the Ark Ltd, Middlesex TW12 2HD
CCLI Song No. 5703586

Un, deux, trois

Je sais compter

Count the objects and write the French word for each number in the correct space.

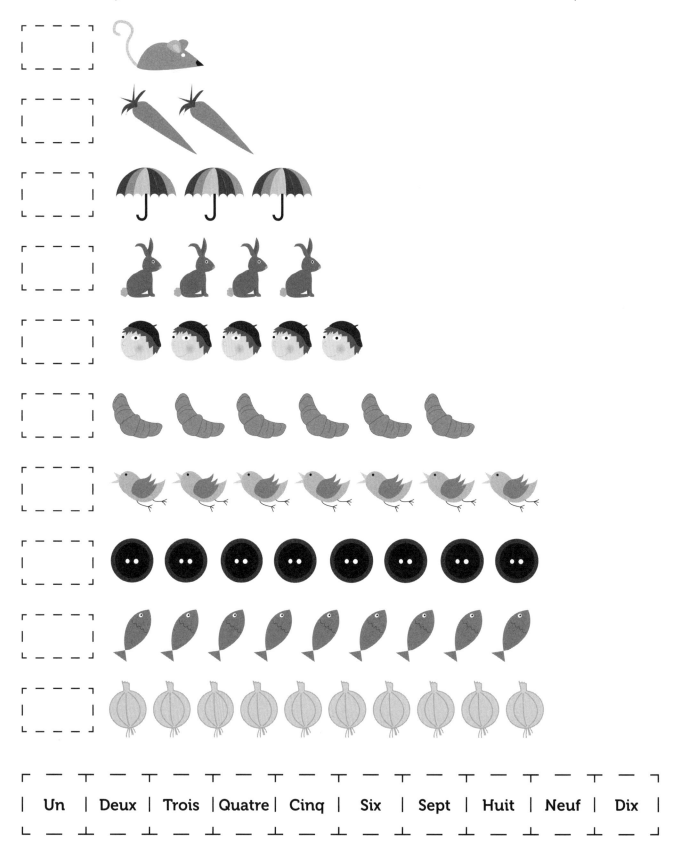

| Un | Deux | Trois | Quatre | Cinq | Six | Sept | Huit | Neuf | Dix |

Lundi, mardi, mercredi

Draw a picture for the different activities you have during the week. Try and find out some of the French words to label your pictures.

	lundi	mardi	mercredi
jeudi	vendredi	samedi	dimanche

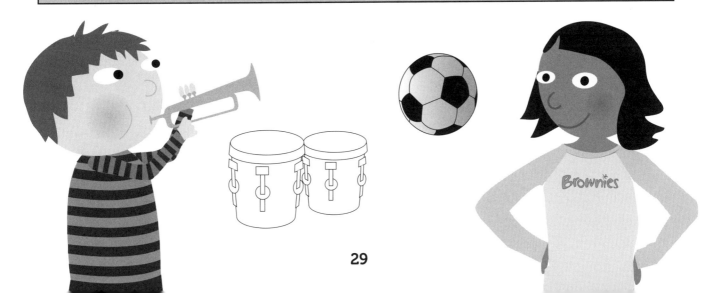

Comment t'appelles-tu?

Draw a picture of yourself, with as much detail as possible, then finish the sentence below.

Je m'appelle...

Dans ma famille

ma famille

Draw a picture of your family and choose from the names below to label each of your family members. Remember to include their name, for example 'Ma sœur Thérèse'.

| Ma mère | Mon père | Ma sœur | Mon frère | et moi |

Circle the correct word to complete the following sentences:

J'ai une deux trois quatre cinq **sœur(s)**.

J'ai un deux trois quatre cinq **frère(s)**.

Je n'ai pas de...(sœurs/frères)

Qu'est-ce que c'est?

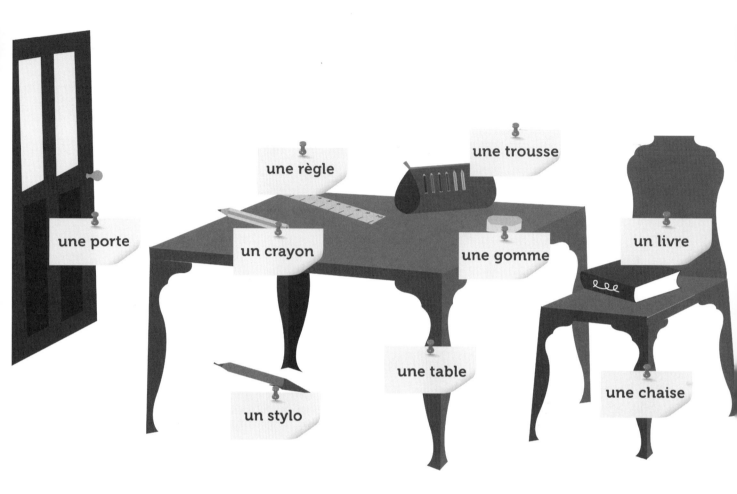

 This game requires two people and a dice. Throw the dice and ask 'Qu'est-ce que c'est? The other person should answer 'C'est un(e) ...' for the picture corresponding to the number thrown. (Choose your own objects to draw in the blank spaces.)

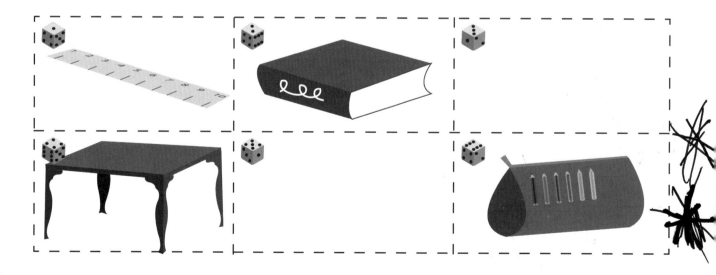

De quelle couleur?

La couleur
des bananes
(jaune)

La couleur
des tomates
(rouge)

La couleur
des oignons
(blanche)

La couleur
des légumes
(verte)

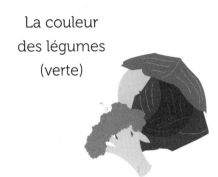

Colour in the pictures and fill in the rest of the sentences with the right French words.

La couleur **des légumes**

est **verte**

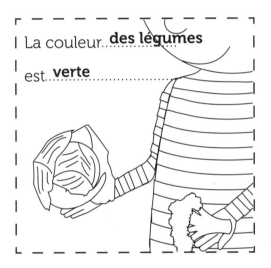

La couleur.............................

est...

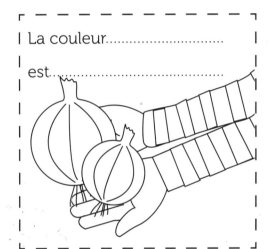

La couleur.............................

est...

La couleur.............................

est...

Fill in each circle with the correct colour.

rouge   noir(e)   jaune   rose   vert(e)   bleu   marron   orange

Mon petit ami bizarre

Design your own 'funny/strange little friend' including as many of each body part as you want. When your friend is complete, count how many eyes, ears, heads, etc. it has and write the number in French under each body-part picture.

Les animaux

Can you find the French name for each animal?

un cheval

une souris

un chien

un lapin

un chat

un dauphin

Draw in your own favourite animal and complete the sentence below:

Je voudrais avoir ....

Tous les jours

Draw a picture in each space to illustrate what is being done every day.

Je me lève

Je me lave

Tous les jours

Je me coiffe

Je me couche

Dans ma poche

Draw a line to connect the correct picture to the correct word

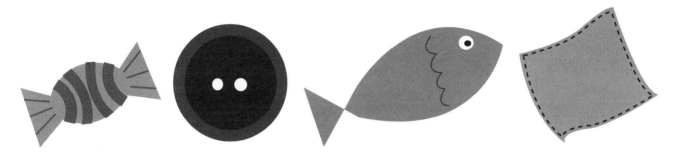

| un poisson | un bonbon | un chiffon | un bouton |

Complete the sentences below

Dans ma poche j'ai un ....

Dans ma poche j'ai deux ....

Dans ma poche j'ai trois ....

Dans ma poche j'ai quatre ....

Extension work

Draw your own pocket filled with other items you have learnt in French. Show your drawing and read out the list of what you have in your pocket.

J'ai perdu mon chapeau!

Colour in the pictures and select the correct words to complete the sentences below.

J'ai.....................mon.....................

J'ai.....................mon.....................

J'ai.....................mon.....................

J'ai.....................mon.....................

chapeau

bateau

lavé

gâteau

perdu

mangé

Où se trouve mon parapluie?

Draw the weather described in each box.

Il pleut	Il neige	Il fait froid

Il fait chaud	Il fait du vent

Quel temps fait-il aujourd'hui?······*What's the weather like today?*

Aujourd'hui, il...

Un, deux, trois

Words and Music by
Mark and Helen Johnson

Gradually getting faster ♩ = 164-232

Un, deux, trois, quatre, cinq, six, sept, huit, neuf et

dix. Un, deux, trois, quatre, cinq, six, sept, huit, neuf et

Harmony part 2°

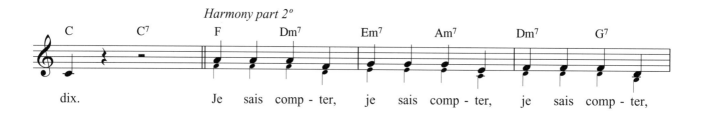

dix. Je sais comp - ter, je sais comp - ter, je sais comp - ter,

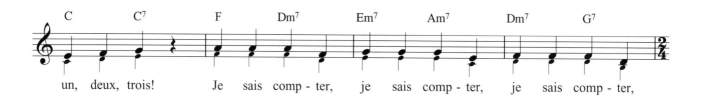

un, deux, trois! Je sais comp - ter, je sais comp - ter, je sais comp - ter,

Faster

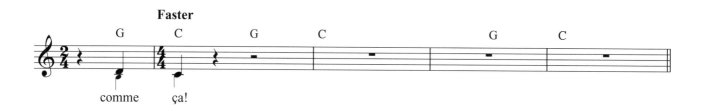

comme ça!

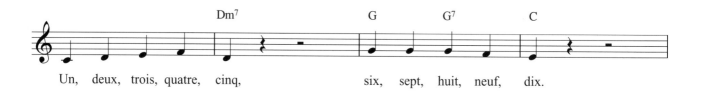

Un, deux, trois, quatre, cinq, six, sept, huit, neuf, dix.

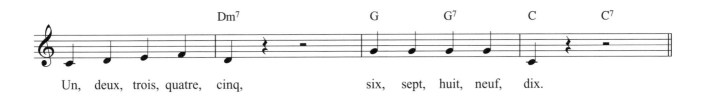

Un, deux, trois, quatre, cinq,   six, sept, huit, neuf, dix.

Je sais comp - ter,   je sais comp - ter,   je sais comp - ter,   un, deux, trois!

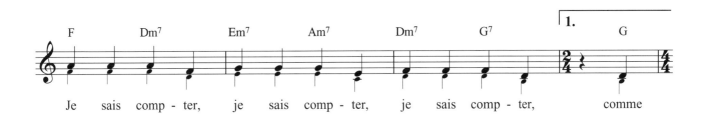

Je sais comp - ter,   je sais comp - ter,   je sais comp - ter,   comme

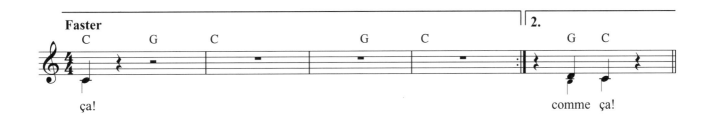

ça!   comme ça!

Je sais comp - ter,   je sais comp - ter,   je sais comp - ter,   un, deux, trois!

Je sais comp - ter,   je sais comp - ter,   je sais comp - ter,   comme ça!

Lundi, mardi, mercredi

Words and Music by
Mark and Helen Johnson

♩ = 80

Lun - di, mar - di, mer - cre - di,___ jeu - di,

ven - dre - di.___ Lun - di, mar - di, mer - cre - di,___ jeu - di, ven - dre - di.___

J'aime beau - coup___ le week - end, same - di, et dim - anche.___

J'aime beau - coup___ le week - end, same - di et dim - anche.___

C'est quel jour au - jourd' - hui?___ Au - jourd' - hui___ c'est mer - cre - di! lun - di!

C'est quel jour au - jourd' - hui?___ Au - jourd' - hui___ c'est mer - cre - di! lun - di!

C'est quel jour au - jourd' - hui?___ Au - jourd' - hui___ c'est mer - cre - di! lun - di!

D.C. (without repeats)

C'est quel jour au - jourd' - hui?___ Au - jourd' - hui___ c'est mer - cre - di! lun - di!

Comment t'appelles-tu?

Words and Music by
Mark and Helen Johnson

Dans ma famille

Words and Music by
Mark and Helen Johnson

Qu'est-ce que c'est?

Words and Music by
Mark and Helen Johnson

De quelle couleur?

Words and Music by
Mark and Helen Johnson

Mon petit ami bizarre

Words and Music by
Mark and Helen Johnson

* Or 'mon petit copain bizarre' (my funny little friend)

Les animaux

Words and Music by
Mark and Helen Johnson

Tous les jours

Words and Music by
Mark and Helen Johnson

Dans ma poche

Words and Music by
Mark and Helen Johnson

1. Dans ma poche j'ai un pois - son!__
3. Dans ma poche j'ai trois bou - tons!__

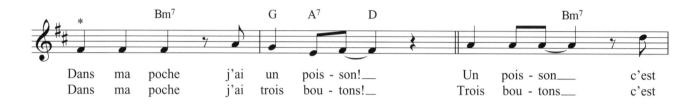

Dans ma poche j'ai un pois - son!__ Un pois - son__ c'est
Dans ma poche j'ai trois bou - tons!__ Trois bou - tons__ c'est

am - us - ant!__ Oh - la - la!___ Quel grand pois - son!__
am - us - ant!__ Oh - la - la!___ Quels grands bou - tons!__

2. Dans ma poche j'ai deux chif - fons!__ Dans ma poche j'ai
4. Dans ma poche j'ai quatre bon - bons!__ Dans ma poche j'ai

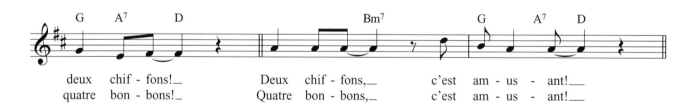

deux chif - fons!__ Deux chif - fons,__ c'est am - us - ant!__
quatre bon - bons!__ Quatre bon - bons,__ c'est am - us - ant!__

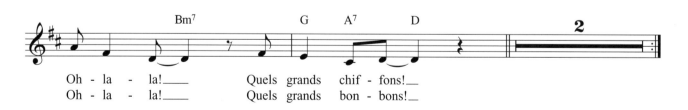

Oh - la - la!___ Quels grands chif - fons!__
Oh - la - la!___ Quels grands bon - bons!__

* If singing as a round, each group should begin as the group before reaches this point. Use first 3 verses only.

J'ai perdu mon chapeau!

Words and Music by
Mark and Helen Johnson

© 2010 Out of the Ark Ltd, Middlesex TW12 2HD   CCLI Song No. 5703579

51

Où se trouve mon parapluie?

Words and Music by
Mark and Helen Johnson

With energy ♩ = 130

1. Il fait froid, auj - ourd' - hui,___ je n'aime pas___ le temps___

___ d'i - ci!___ Quand il pleut, quel - qu'un dit,___

'Où se trouve mon par - a - pluie?!'

2. Il fait chaud, auj - ourd' - hui,___ J'aime beau - coup___ le temps___

___ d'i - ci.___ Quand il pleut, quel - qu'un dit,___

'Où se trouve___ mon par - a - pluie?!'___

B E B E B E B E B

3. Il fait froid, auj - ourd'- hui,___ Je n'aime pas___ le temps___

E B E B E B

___ d'i - ci!___ Quand il pleut, quel - qu'un dit,___

E B E B E B **2** C F C

'Où se trouve_ mon par - a - pluie?!' 4. Il fait chaud,

F C F C F C F C

auj - ourd'- hui,___ J'aime beau - coup___ le temps___ d'i - ci.___

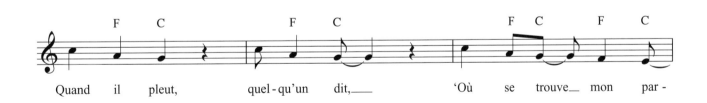

F C F C F C F C

Quand il pleut, quel - qu'un dit,___ 'Où se trouve_ mon par -

E⁷ Am F C F C G⁷ C

- a - pluie?!___ Où se trouve_ mon par - a - pluie?!'___

A

aimer (verb)	*to like*
j'aime	*I like*
j'aime beaucoup	*I really like*
l'**ami(e)**	*friend*
amusant	*funny*
l'**animal**	*animal*
les **animaux**	*animals*
appeler (verb)	*to call*
s'appeler	*to be called*
je m'appelle	*my name is*
aujourd'hui	*today*
avoir (verb)	*to have*

B

la **banane**	*banana*
le **bateau**	*boat*
beaucoup	*a lot/much*
bizarre	*funny/strange*
blanc(he)	*white*
bleu	*blue*
le **bonbon**	*sweet*
la **bouche**	*mouth*
le **bouton**	*button*
le **bras**	*arm*

C

Ça va très bien, merci!	*I'm very well, thank you*
la **carotte**	*carrot*
la **chaise**	*chair*
le **chapeau**	*hat*
le **chat**	*cat*
chaud	*hot*
le **cheval**	*horse*
le **chien**	*dog*
le **chiffon**	*duster*
cinq	*five*
se **coiffer**	*to do one's hair*
je me **coiffe**	*I do my hair*
Comment ça va?	*How are you?*
Comment t'appelles-tu? (girl and boy)	*What's your name?*
se **coucher**	*to go to bed*
je me **couche**	*I go to bed*
la **couleur**	*colour*
le **crayon**	*pencil*

D

dans	*in*
le **dauphin**	*dolphin*
la **dent**	*tooth*
deux	*two*
dimanche	*Sunday*
dire (verb)	*to say*
je dirais	*I would say*
dis-le moi	*tell me*
dix	*ten*

E

et ··· *and*

F

la **famille** ································ *family*
faux ······································· *false*
la **framboise** ························· *raspberry*
le **frère** ······························· *brother*
froid ······································ *cold*

G

le **gâteau** ····························· *cake*
la **gomme** ····························· *rubber*
grand(e) ································· *big*

H

huit ······································· *eight*

I

ici ··· *here*
il fait froid ···························· *it's cold*

J

la **jambe** ······························· *leg*
jaune ···································· *yellow*
Je ·· *I*
jeudi ····································· *Thursday*
le **jour** ································· *day*

L

le **lapin** ······························· *rabbit*
laver (verb) ···························· *to wash*
  se laver ···················· *to wash (oneself)*
  je me lave ················· *I wash (myself)*
le **légume** ····························· *vegetable*
lever (verb) ···························· *to raise*
  se lever ······················ *to get up*
  je me lève ·················· *I get up*
le **livre** ································ *book*
lundi ····································· *Monday*

M

ma/mon/mes ······················ *my*
la **main** ································ *hand*
mardi ···································· *Tuesday*
marron ·································· *brown*
merci ···································· *thank you*
mercredi ······························· *Wednesday*
la **mère** ································ *mother*
moi ······································· *me*
mon/ma/mes ······················ *my*
le **monde** ····························· *world*

N

neuf ······································ *nine*
noir(e) ··································· *black*

O

l'**oignon**(m) ························· *onion*
orange (adj) ···························· *orange*
l'**orange**(f) ··························· *orange*
l'**oreille**(f) ···························· *ear*

55

P

le **parapluie**	umbrella
penser (verb)	to think
perdre (verb)	to lose
j'ai perdu	I have lost
le **père**	father
petit(e)	small
le **pied**	foot
la **pluie**	rain
il **pleut**	it's raining
la **poche**	pocket
le **poisson**	fish
la **porte**	door

Q

qu'en pensez-vous?	what do you think?
quand	when
quatre	four
quel(le)	which/what

R

la **règle**	ruler
rencontrer (verb)	to meet
rose	pink
rouge	red

S

s'il te plaît	please (when talking amongst friends/to children)
s'il vous plaît	please (more formal, for use when talking to an adult)
samedi	Saturday
sept	seven
six	six
la **soeur**	sister
la **souris**	mouse
le **stylo**	pen
surtout	especially

T

la **table**	table
le **temps**	weather
la **tête**	head
toi	you
la **tomate**	tomato
tous les jours	every day
trois	three
la **trousse**	pencil case
trouver (verb)	to find
se trouver	to be situated

U

un(e)	a/one

V

vendredi	Friday
vert(e)	green
violet	purple
voila!	there is/there it is
vouloir (verb)	to want
je voudrais	I would like
vrai	true

W

le **weekend**	weekend

Y

les **yeux**	eyes
(but **un oeil**	an eye)